FILM SONGS

ISBN 978-1-61774-204-0

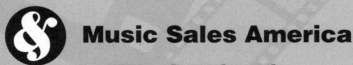

Music Sales America

Exclusively Distributed By
HAL•LEONARD®
CORPORATION
7777 W. BLUEMOUND RD. P.O. BOX 13819 MILWAUKEE, WI 53213

Visit Hal Leonard Online at
www.halleonard.com

AGAINST ALL ODDS
(Take a Look at Me Now)
from AGAINST ALL ODDS

Words and Music by
PHIL COLLINS

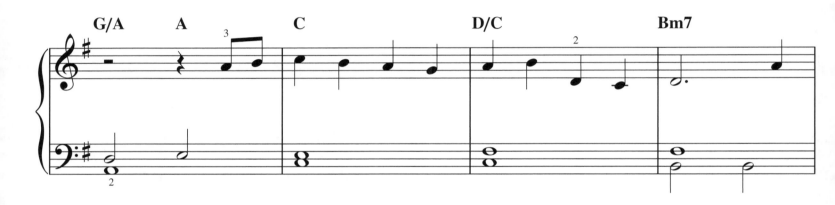

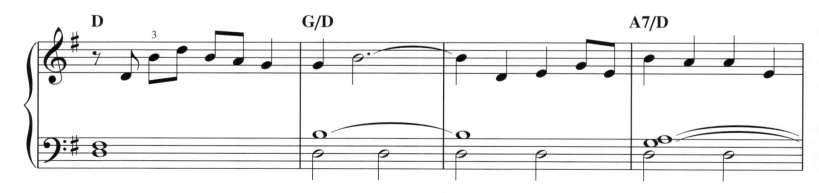

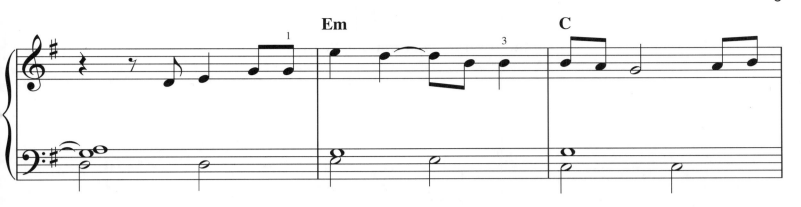

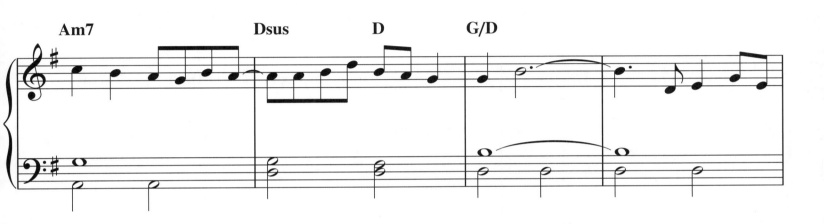

ALFIE
Theme from the Paramount Picture ALFIE

Words by HAL DAVID
Music by BURT BACHARACH

BEYOND THE SEA

featured in the Walt Disney/Pixar Film FINDING NEMO

Lyrics by JACK LAWRENCE
Music by CHARLES TRENET and ALBERT LASRY
Original French Lyric to "La Mer" by CHARLES TRENET

CAN YOU FEEL THE LOVE TONIGHT

from Walt Disney Pictures' THE LION KING

Music by ELTON JOHN
Lyrics by TIM RICE

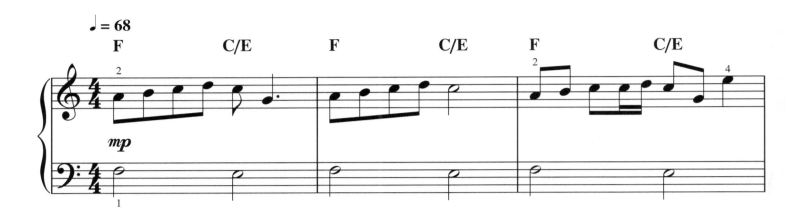

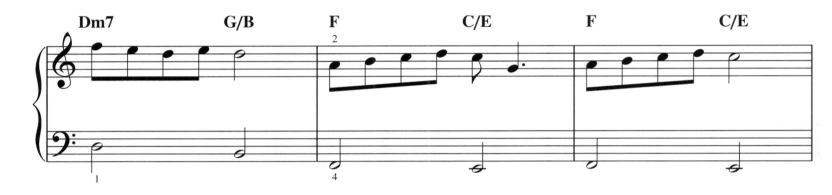

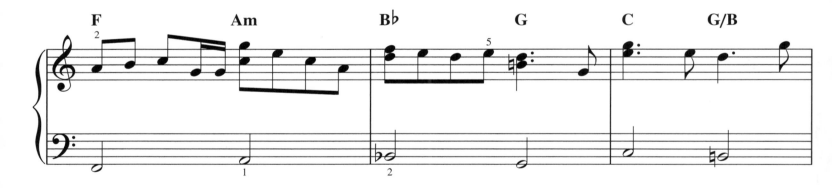

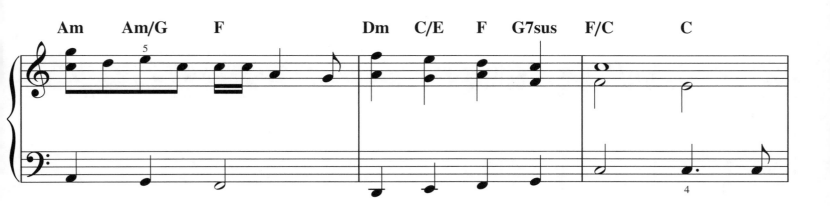

COME WHAT MAY

from the Motion Picture MOULIN ROUGE

Words and Music by
DAVID BAERWALD

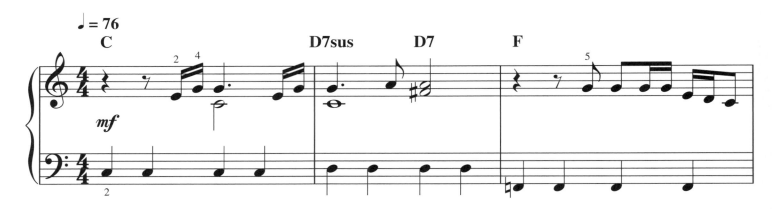

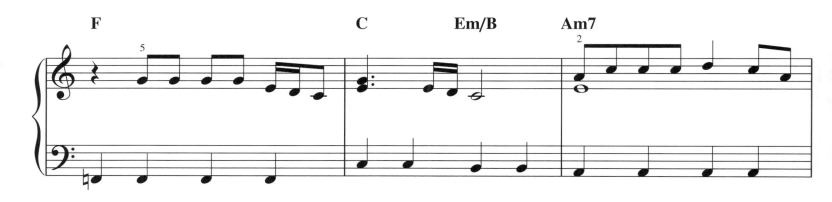

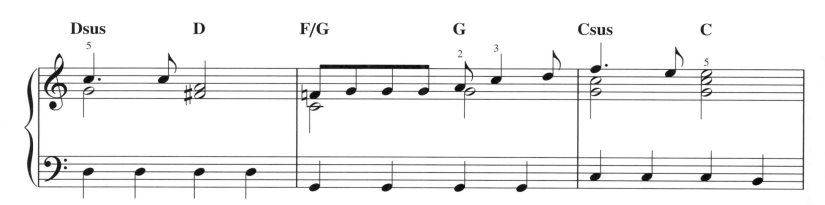

THEME FROM E.T.
(The Extra-Terrestrial)
from the Universal Picture E.T. (THE EXTRA-TERRESTRIAL)

Music By JOHN WILLIAMS

I WILL ALWAYS LOVE YOU

featured in THE BODYGUARD

Words and Music by
DOLLY PARTON

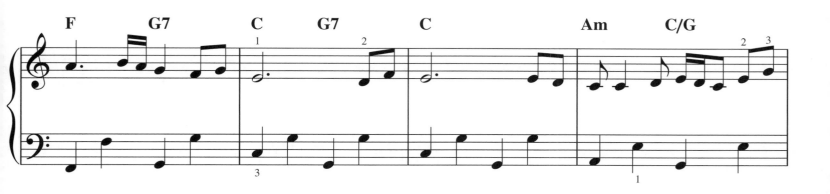

(Everything I Do)
I DO IT FOR YOU

from the Motion Picture ROBIN HOOD: PRINCE OF THIEVES

Written by MICHAEL KAMEN

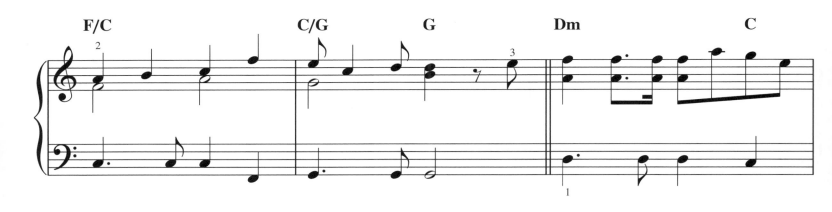

HOPELESSLY DEVOTED TO YOU

from GREASE

Words and Music by
JOHN FARRAR

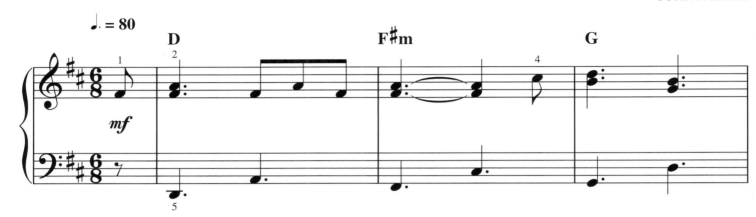

HOW DEEP IS YOUR LOVE

from the Motion Picture SATURDAY NIGHT FEVER

Words and Music by BARRY GIBB,
ROBIN GIBB and MAURICE GIBB

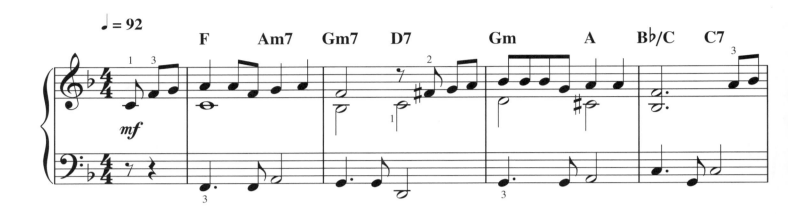

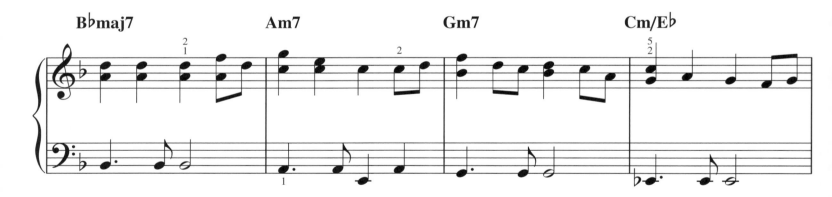

LOVE IS ALL AROUND

featured on the Motion Picture Soundtrack FOUR WEDDINGS AND A FUNERAL

Words and Music by
REG PRESLEY

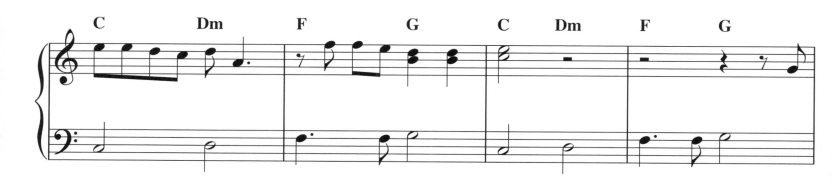

MRS. ROBINSON
from THE GRADUATE

Words and Music by
PAUL SIMON

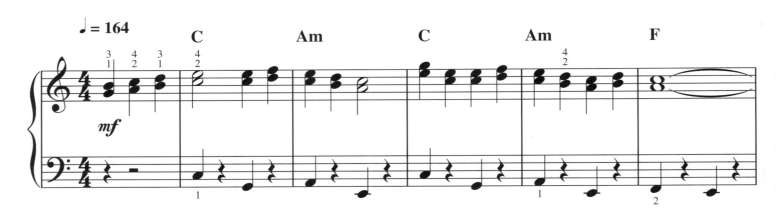

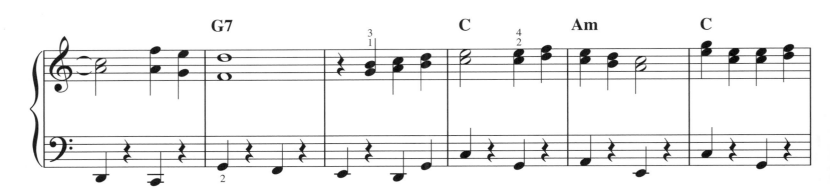

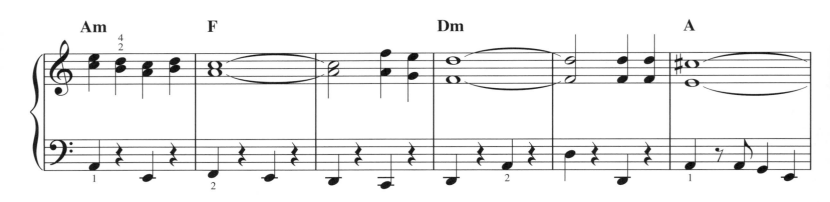

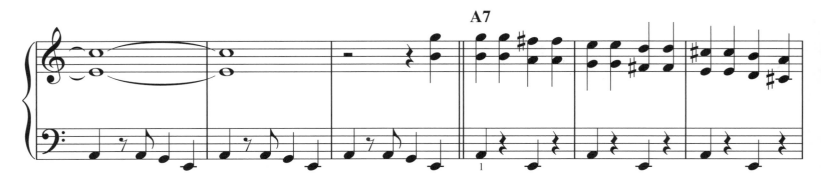

MOON RIVER

from the Paramount Picture BREAKFAST AT TIFFANY'S

Words by JOHNNY MERCER
Music by HENRY MANCINI

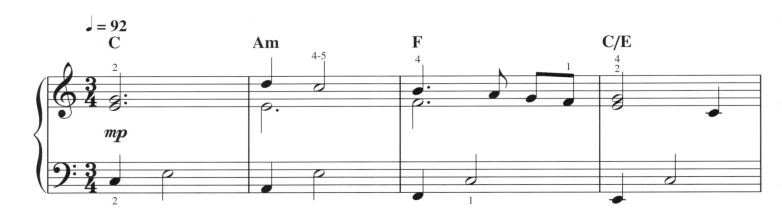

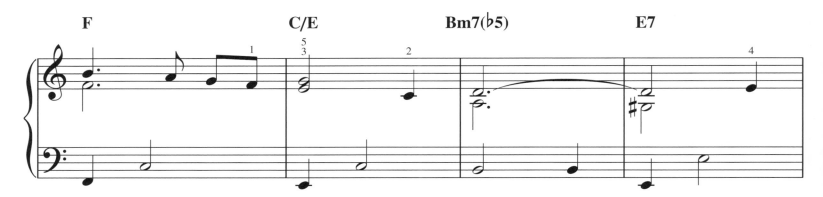

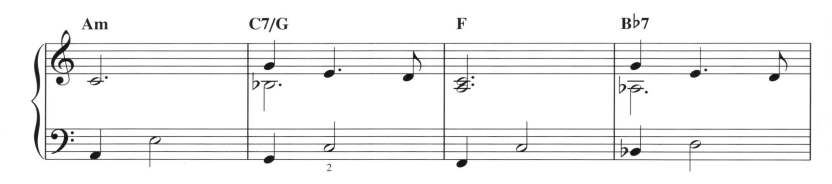

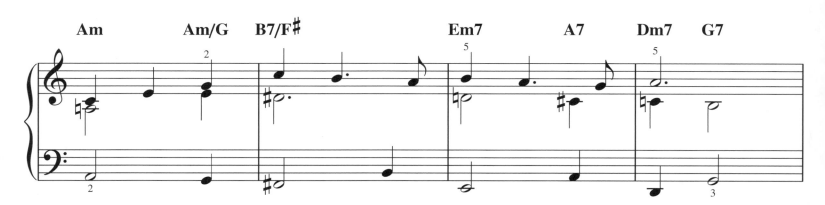

MY HEART WILL GO ON

(Love Theme from 'Titanic')

from the Paramount and Twentieth Century Fox Motion Picture TITANIC

Music by JAMES HORNER
Lyric by WILL JENNINGS

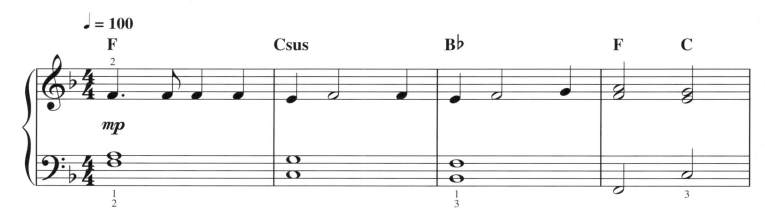

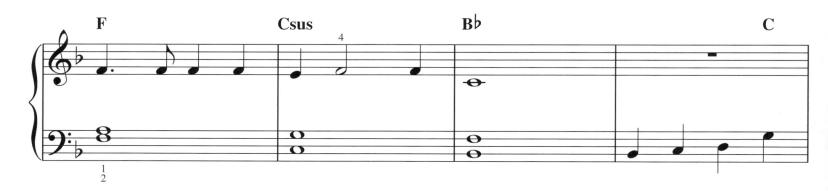

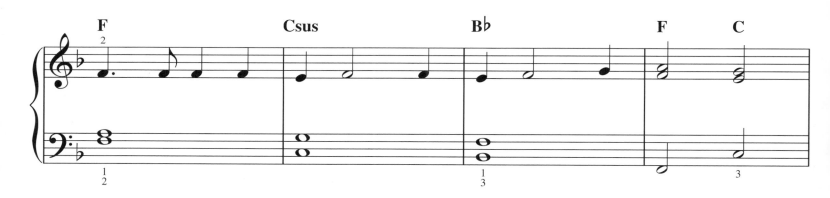

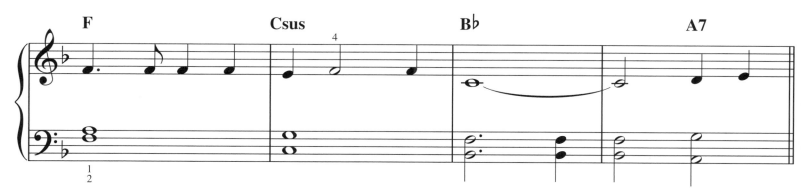

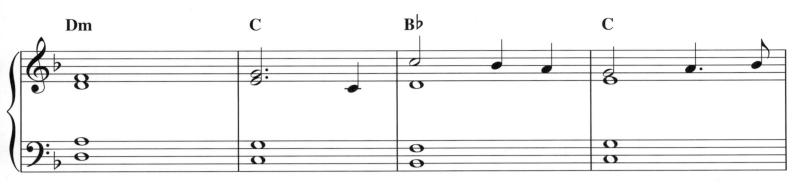

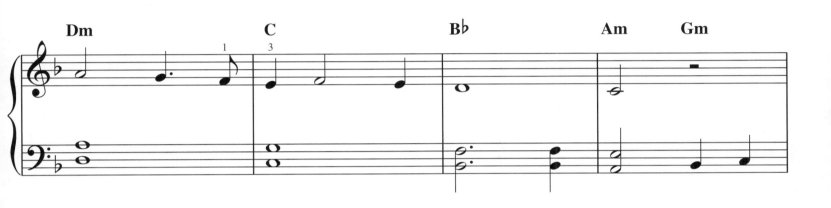

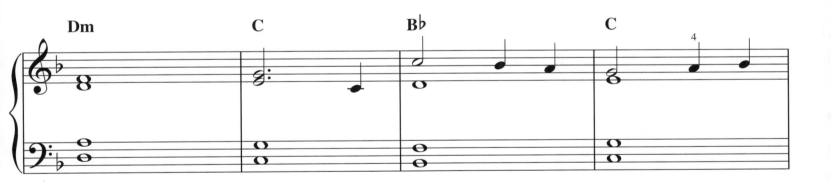

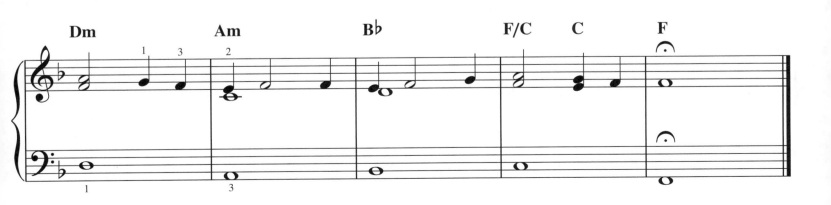

OH, PRETTY WOMAN

featured in the Motion Picture PRETTY WOMAN

Words and Music by ROY ORBISON
and BILL DEES

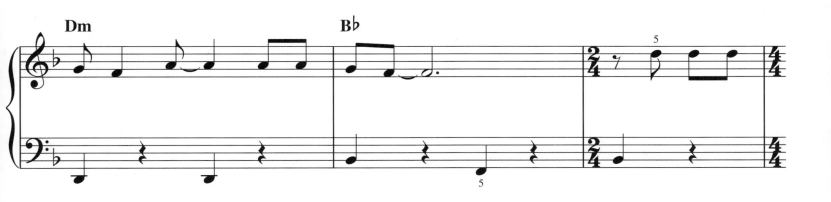

RAINDROPS KEEP FALLIN'
ON MY HEAD

from BUTCH CASSIDY AND THE SUNDANCE KID

Lyric by HAL DAVID
Music by BURT BACHARACH

31

THE RIVER KWAI MARCH
from THE BRIDGE ON THE RIVER KWAI

By MALCOLM ARNOLD

THEME FROM "SCHINDLER'S LIST"

from the Universal Motion Picture SCHINDLER'S LIST

Music by JOHN WILLIAMS

SON-OF-A-PREACHER MAN

Words and Music by JOHN HURLEY
and RONNIE WILKINS

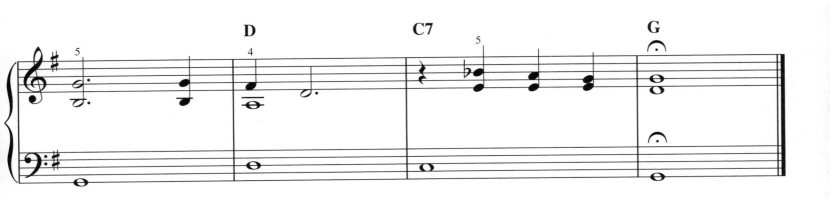

SPEAK SOFTLY, LOVE

(Love Theme)
from the Paramount Picture THE GODFATHER

Words by LARRY KUSIK
Music by NINO ROTA

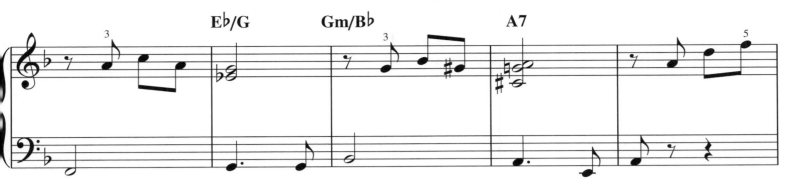

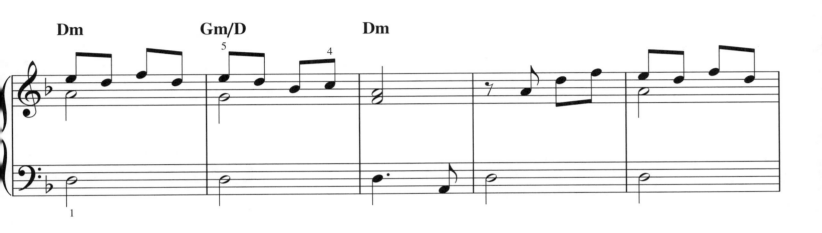

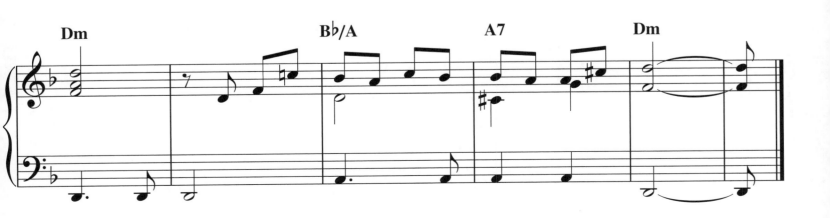

TAKE MY BREATH AWAY

(Love Theme)

from the Paramount Picture TOP GUN

Words and Music by GIORGIO MORODER
and TOM WHITLOCK

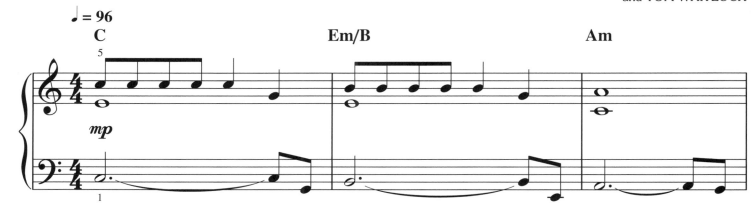

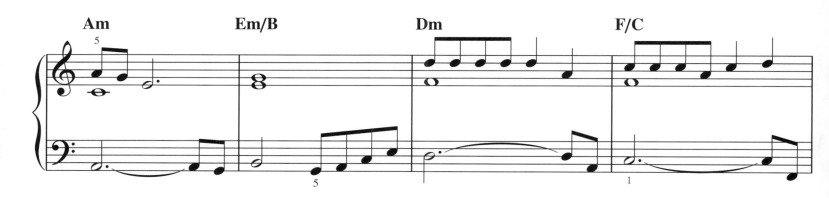

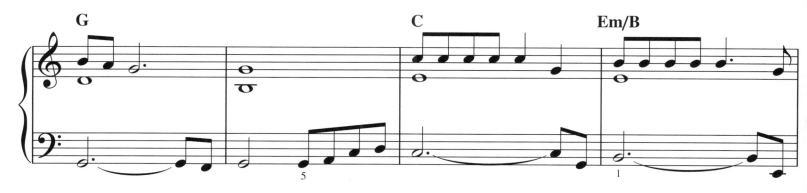

UNCHAINED MELODY

from the Motion Picture UNCHAINED
featured in the Motion Picture GHOST

Lyric by HY ZARET
Music by ALEX NORTH

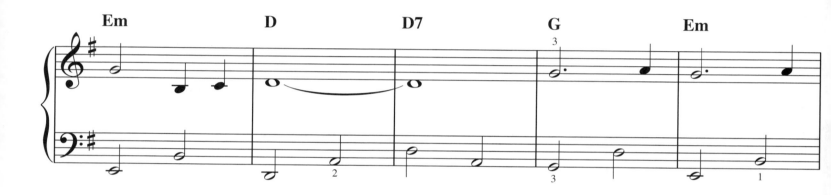

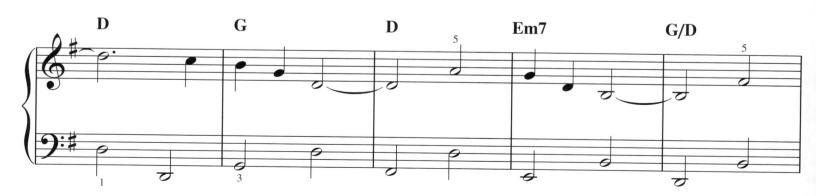

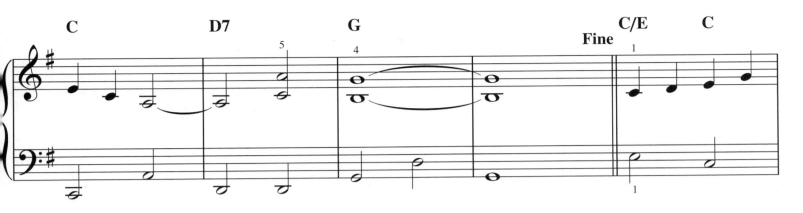

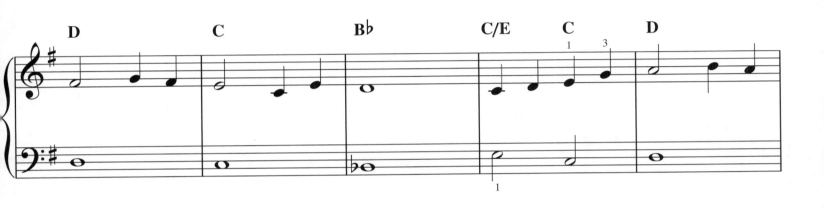

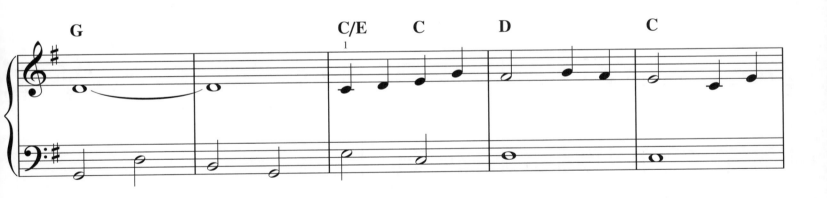

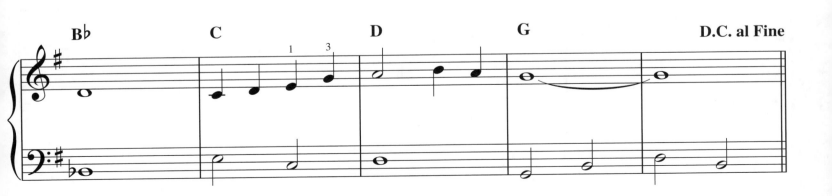

UP WHERE WE BELONG

from the Paramount Picture AN OFFICER AND A GENTLEMAN

Words by WILL JENNINGS
Music by BUFFY SAINTE-MARIE
and JACK NITZSCHE

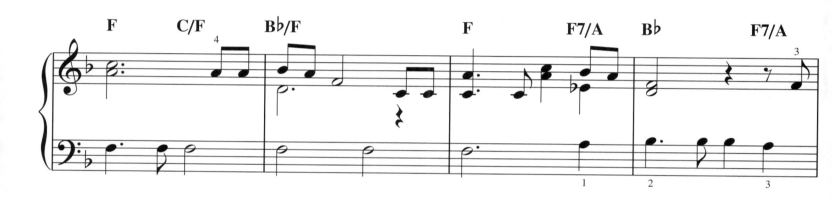

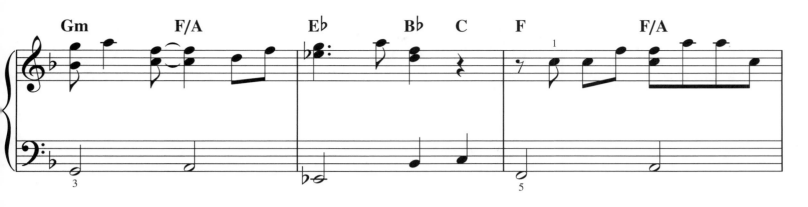

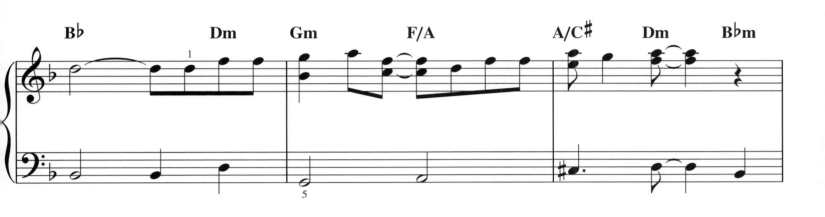

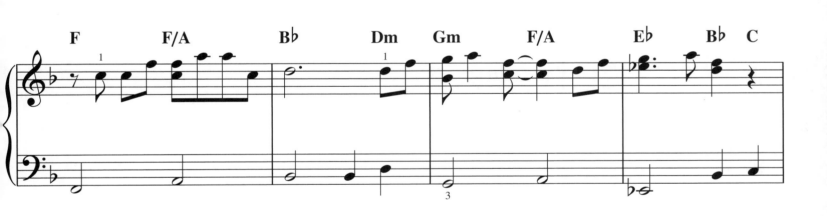

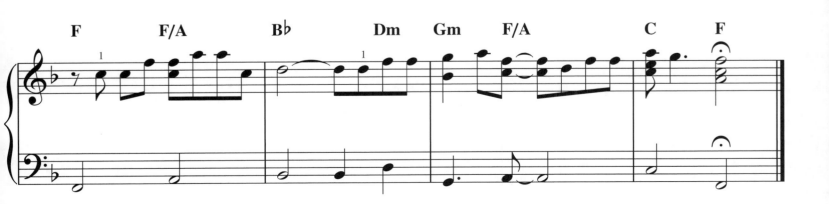